becoming
me
a story of creation

by Martin Boroson
paintings by Christopher Gilvan-Cartwright

Kanzeon Press
Totnes, Devon, England

Design: Martin Boroson and ThiruMoolar Devar, based on the original design by Sarah Slack.
Production Supervision: Teri Rider

Second Edition
Published by Kanzeon Press, 2022
Totnes, Devon, England
kanzeonpress.com

First Edition
Published in Great Britain in 2000 by
Frances Lincoln Children's Books
Published in the United States in 2000 by
Skylight Paths

Publisher's Cataloging-in-Publication Data
Names: Boroson, Martin, author. | Gilvan-Cartwright, Christopher, illustrator.
Title: Becoming me : a story of creation / written by Martin Boroson ; illustrated by Christopher Gilvan-Cartwright.
Description: Second edition. | Totnes, Devon, England : Kanzeon Press, [2022] | "First edition published in Great Britain in 2000 by Frances Lincoln Children's Books; first published in the United States in 2000 by Skylight Paths."--Title page verso. | Audience: Ages four to forever. | Summary: "Becoming Me" presents the mystical view of creation as a playful process of self discovery in the form of a children's story, told from the divine point-of-view.--Publisher.
Identifiers: ISBN: 979-8-9869849-0-2 (hardback) | 979-8-9869849-1-9 (paperback) | 979-8-9869849-2-6 (eBook)
Subjects: LCSH: Creation. | Creation--Juvenile literature. | Spirituality. | Spirituality--Juvenile literature. | Mysticism. | Self-consciousness (Awareness). | Love. | Inspiration. | Ecology. | Mind and body. | Transpersonal psychology. | Self-actualization (Psychology). | Compassion. | Play. | Philosophy. | CYAC: Creation. | Spirituality. | Love. | LCGFT: Fables. | BISAC: RELIGION / Inspirational. | BODY, MIND & SPIRIT / Mysticism. | JUVENILE FICTION / Legends, Myths, Fables / General. | RELIGION / Spirituality.
Classification: LCC: BL226 .B67 2022 | DDC: 231.7/65--dc23

Printed in USA

For Andrew, Toɓs, and the fambly, with my love. M.B.

For Isobel, Bluebell, and Eddie, with much love. C.G-C.

Once upon
a time ...

I was.

There was nobody who knew that I was ...

But I was.

I liked to make myself into different shapes.

Lots of different shapes — all me.

Everywhere I looked, there was only me.

I must be very big.

I played by myself for ages.

It seemed like forever.

Then I started to get lonely.

I wanted someone else to play with,

someone who wasn't ME.

So I took a deep breath, gathered all my

strength together, and squeezed really hard.

I started to feel dizzy.

It felt like I was falling.

And then suddenly, in a big burst,

I became ...

something ELSE!

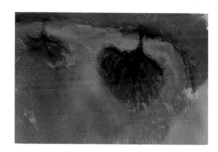

This was so much fun,
I did it again and again,
lots of different ways.
I do it all the time now.

I can become all kinds of things,
things that ...

grow   and swim

and fly

and crawl

and run.

One day, I squeezed extra hard.
I **pushed** and I **pushed** and I **pushed**,
and then all of a sudden, I became ...

YOU

What is this thing I'm in?
Just one moment ago, I was SO BIG,
and now I'm SO little.
It's like I'm all wrapped up in love.

But as soon as I become you,
you forget that you're me.

In time, you forget all about me.

Every so often, you wonder who you are.
And I'm right here, reminding you.

I'm always busy now, cheering you on.

I like it best when you discover me.
Then we play together, you and I.

And sometimes you realize
that you ARE me.

Sometimes you forget
that everything else
is me too.

But even then ...

I still love you ...

little ME.

Biographies

Martin Boroson is an executive coach, psychotherapist, and a priest in the Hollow Bones Rinzai Zen Order. He is Dean of Transformational Programs at Mobius Executive Leadership and co-founder of The One Moment Company, a consultancy that helps organizations solve their 'time problem'. A graduate of Yale College and the Yale School of Management, he is the creator of the One-Moment Meditation® app and workforce training programs, and author of *One-Moment Meditation: Stillness for People on the Go.*

martinboroson.com

Christopher Gilvan-Cartwright, aka The Baron Gilvan, is a graduate of Central Saint Martins. He was selected for Bloomberg New Contemporaries and was the first Artist in Residence at Glyndebourne Opera House. As a winner of the Royal Over-Seas League Travel Scholarship, he travelled to paint in India and Nepal. On his return he was commissioned to design the logos for the BBC Proms for two seasons. He has exhibited widely and performed at the Towner Museum of Contemporary Art and Hastings Contemporary.

thebarongilvan.com

Acknowledgements

The gestation of this story, over many years, would not have been possible without the work of Stanislav and Christina Grof and my friends who were influenced by them, including Barbara Dickey, Martin Duffy, Barbara Egan, Jean Farrell, and Anne Fitzmaurice. Above all, I am grateful to Nienke Merbis, who held space for the birth of this story with such wisdom and love. As I nurtured the story, I was supported by the writings of Ken Wilber, Huston Smith, Ervin Laszlo, and Stan Grof.

For the first edition of this book, I was blessed to find the team at Frances Lincoln, Ltd. who treated this story with great delicacy and introduced me to Chris, already working on similar themes; Chris has been such a generous collaborator—twice. Many angels then helped me produce this new edition, including Christiaan Jörg, Meghan Ferrin, Teri Rider, Vicky Likens, Jason Browning, Kirsty Gilbert-Browning, Grigol Abashidze, and ThiruMoolar Devar.

For their support on this project in many ways—from editorial and design advice to friendship, patience, and love—my deep thanks to Carmel Moore, Barbara Boroson, Andrew Dodd, Joe Rutt, and my parents, Florence and Louis Boroson. A special thank you to my visionary friend, Amy Fox, who said yes … and in that moment, crystallized this. — M.B.

For courses, events, and reading group guides, visit: **becomingme.com**